# The Va

Richard Stockham

Alpha Editions

This edition published in 2024

ISBN : 9789362093745

Design and Setting By
**Alpha Editions**
www.alphaedis.com
Email - info@alphaedis.com

As per information held with us this book is in Public Domain. This book is a reproduction of an important historical work. Alpha Editions uses the best technology to reproduce historical work in the same manner it was first published to preserve its original nature. Any marks or number seen are left intentionally to preserve its true form.

# THE VALLEY

### –By Richard Stockham

*If you can't find it countless millions of miles in space, come back to Earth. You might find it just on the other side of the fence—where the grass is always greener.*

---

The Ship dove into Earth's sea of atmosphere like a great, silver fish.

Inside the ship, a man and woman stood looking down at the expanse of land that curved away to a growing horizon. They saw the yellow ground cracked like a dried skin; and the polished stone of the mountains and the seas that were shrunken away in the dust. And they saw how the city circled the sea, as a circle of men surround a water hole in a desert under a blazing sun.

The ship's radio cried out. "You've made it! Thank God! You've made it!"

Another voice, shaking, said, "President—Davis is—overwhelmed. He can't go on. On his behalf and on behalf of all the people—with our hope that was almost dead, we greet you." A pause. "Please come in!"

The voice was silent. The air screamed against the hull of the ship.

"I can't tell them," said the man.

"Please come in!" said the radio. "Do you hear me?"

The woman looked up at the man. "You've got to Michael!"

"Two thousand years. From one end of the galaxy to the other. Not one grain of dust we can live on. Just Earth. And it's burned to a cinder."

A note of hysteria stabbed into the radio voice. "Are you all right? Stand by! We're sending a rescue ship."

"They've got a right to know what we've found," said the woman. "They sent us out. They've waited so long—."

He stared into space. "It's hopeless. If we'd found another planet they could live on, they'd do the same as they've done here."

He touched the tiny golden locket that hung around his neck. "Right now, I could press this and scratch myself and the whole farce would be over."

"No. A thousand of us died. You've got to think of them."

"We'll go back out into space," he said. "It's clean out there. I'm tired. Two thousand years of reincarnation."

She spoke softly. "We've been together for a long time. I've loved you. I've asked very little. But I need to stay on Earth. Please, Michael."

He looked at her for a moment. Then he flipped a switch. "Milky Way to Earth. Never mind the rescue ship. We're all right. We're coming in."

---

The great, white ship settled to Earth that was like a plain after flood waters have drained away.

The man and woman came out into the blazing sunlight.

A shout, like the crashing of a thousand surfs, rose and broke over them. The man and woman descended the gang-plank toward the officials gathered on the platform. They glanced around at the massed field of white faces beneath them; saw those same faces that had been turned toward them two thousand years past; remembered the cheers and the cries that had crashed around them then, as they and the thousand had stood before the towering spires of the ships, before the takeoff.

And, as then, there were no children among the milling, grasping throng. Only the same clutching hands and voices and arms, asking for an answer, a salvation, a happy end.

Now the officials gathered around the man and the woman, and spoke to them in voices of reverence.

A microphone was thrust into Michael's hand with the whispered admonition to tell the people of the great new life waiting for them, open and green and moist, on a virgin planet.

The cries of the people were slipping away and a stillness growing like an ocean calm and, within it, the sound of the pumps, throbbing, sucking the water from the seas.

And then Michael's voice, "The thousand who left with us are dead. For some time we've known the other planets in our solar system were uninhabitable. Now we've been from one end of the galaxy to the other. And this is what we've found.... We were given Earth. There's no place else for us. The rest of the planets in the galaxy were given to others. There's no place else for them. We've all had a chance to make the best of Earth. Instead we've made the worst of it. So we're here to stay—and die." He handed the microphone back.

The silence did not change.

The President grasped Michael's arm. "What're you saying?"

A buzzing rose up from the people like that of a swarm of frightened bees. The sea of white faces swayed and their voices began to cry. The din and motion held, long and drawn out, with a wail now and a fluttering beneath it.

Michael and the woman stood above them in the center of the pale, hovering faces of the officials.

"Good God," said the President. "You've got to tell them what you said isn't true!"

"We've been searching two thousand years for a truth," said Michael. "A thousand of us have died finding it. I've told it. That's the way it's got to be."

The President swayed, took the microphone in his hands.

"There's been some mistake!" he cried. "Go back to the pumps and the distilleries! Go back to the water vats and the gardens and the flocks! Go back! Work and wait! We'll get the full truth to you. Everything's going to be *all right!*"

Obediently the mass of faces separated, as though they were being spun away on a whirling disk. Michael and the woman were swallowed up, like pebbles inside a closing hand, and carried away from the great, white ship.

They ushered the man and woman into the beamed and paneled council chambers and sat them in thick chairs before the wall of polished wood desks across which stared the line of faces, silent and waiting. And on a far wall, facing them all, hung a silver screen, fifty feet square.

The President stood. "Members of the council." He paused. "As you heard, they report—complete failure." He turned to Michael. "And now, the proof."

Michael stood beside the motion picture projector, close to his chair. The lights dimmed. There was only the sound of the pumps throbbing in the darkness close and far away, above and beneath and all around. Suddenly on the screen appeared an endless depth of blackness filled with a mass of glowing white, which extended into the room around the watching people, seeming to touch them and then spreading, like an ocean, farther away and out and out into an endless distance.

Now streaks of yellow fire shot into the picture, like a swarm of lightning bugs, the thin sharp nosed shadows of space ships, hurtling, like comets, toward the clustered star smear. And then silent thoughts flashed from the screen into the minds of the spectators; of time passing in months, years and centuries, passing and passing until they themselves seemed to be rushing and rushing into the blackness toward blinding balls of white light, the size of moons.

The dark shapes of smaller spheres circling the blinding ones moved forward into the picture; red, blue, green, yellow, purple and many mixtures of all these, and then one planet filled the screen, seeming to be inflated, like a balloon, into a shining red ball. There was a razor edge of horizon then and pink sky and an expanse of crimson. Flat, yellow creatures lay all around, expanding and contracting. A roaring rose and fell like the roaring of a million winds. Then fear flowed out of the picture into the minds of the watchers so that they gasped and cringed, and a silent voice told them that the atmosphere of this planet would disintegrate a human being.

Now the red ball seemed to pull away from them into the blackness and the blinding balls of light, and all around could be seen the streaks of rocket flame shooting away in all directions.

Suddenly a flash cut the blackness, like the flare of a match, and died, and the watchers caught from the screen the awareness of the death of a ship.

They were also aware of the rushing of time through centuries and they saw the streaking rocket flames and planets rushing at them; saw creatures in squares and circles, in threads wriggling, in lumps and blobs, rolling jumping and crawling; saw them in cloud forms whisking about, changing their shapes, and in flowing wavelets of water. They saw creatures hopping about on one leg and others crawling at incredible speeds on a thousand; saw some with all the numbers of legs and arms in between; and were aware of creatures that were there but invisible.

And those watching the screen on which time and distance were a compressed and distilled kaleidoscope, saw planet after planet and thousands at a time; heard strange noises; rasping and roaring, clinks and whistles, screams and crying, sighing and moaning. And they were aware through all this of atmosphere and ground inimical to man, some that would evaporate at the touch of a human body, or would burst into flame, or swallow, or turn from liquid to solid or solid to liquid. They saw and heard chemical analyses, were aware of this ocean of blackness and clouds of white through which man might move, and must ever move, because he could live only upon this floating dust speck that was Earth.

The picture faded in, close to one of the long, needle nosed crafts, showing inside, a man and a woman. Time was telescoped again while the man cut a tiny piece of scar tissue from his arm and that of the woman, put them in bottles and set them into compartments where solutions dripped rhythmically into the bottles, the temperature was held at that of the human body, and synthetic sunlight focused upon them from many pencil like tubes.

The watchers in the council chamber saw the bits of tissue swell into human embryos in a few seconds, and grow arms and legs and faces and extend themselves into babies. Saw them taken from the bottles and cared for, and become replicas of the man and woman controlling the ship, who, all this time were aging, until life went out of their bodies. Then the ones who had been the scar tissue disintegrated them in the coffin-like tubes and let their dust be sucked out into space—all this through millions of miles and a hundred years, compressed for the watchers into sixty seconds and a few feet of space.

Instantly there was black space on the screen again, with the fingers of flame pointing out behind the dark bodies of the ships.

And then the spectators saw one ship shudder and swerve into a blazing, bluish white star, like a gnat flying into a white hot poker; saw another drop away and away, out and out into the blackness past the swirling white rim of the galaxy, and sink into a dark nothingness.

Great balls of rock showered like hail onto other ships, smashing them into grotesque tin cans. The stream of fire at the tail of another ship suddenly died and the ship floated into an orbit around a great, yellow planet, ten times the size of Jupiter, then was sucked into it. Another burst like a bomb, flinging a man and woman out into the darkness, where they hung suspended, frozen into statues, like bodies drowned in the depths of an Arctic sea.

At this instant from the watching council, there were screams of horror and voices crying out, "Shut it off! Shut it off!" There was a moving about in the darkness. Murmurs and harsh cries of disapproval grew in volume.

Another ship in the picture was split down the side by a meteor and the bodies inside were impaled on jagged blades of steel, the contorted, bloody faces lighted by bursts of flame. And the screams and cries of the spectators rose higher, "Shut it off.... Oh Lord...."

Lights flashed through the room and the picture died.

---

Michael and Mary, both staring, saw, along the line of desks, the agonized faces, some staring like white stones, others hidden in clutching fingers, as though they had been confronted by a Medusa. There was the sound of heavy breathing that mixed with the throbbing of the pumps. The President held tightly to the edges of his desk to quiet his trembling.

"There—there've been changes," he said, "since you've been out in space. There isn't a person on Earth who's seen a violent death for hundreds of years."

Michael faced him, frowning. "I don't follow you."

"Dying violently happened so seldom on Earth that, after a long time, the sight of it began to drive some people mad. And then one day a man was struck by one of the ground cars and *everyone* who saw it went insane. Since then we've eliminated accidents, even the idea. Now, no one is aware that death by violence is even a possibility."

"I'm sorry," said Michael, "we've been so close to violent death for so long.... What you've seen is part of the proof you asked for."

"What you showed us was a picture," said the President. "If it had been real, we'd all be insane by now. If it were shown to the people there'd be mass hysteria."

"But even if we'd found another habitable planet, getting to it would involve just what we've shown you. Maybe only a tenth of the people who left Earth, or a hundredth, would ever reach a destination out in space."

"We couldn't tolerate such a possibility," said the President gravely. "We'd have to find a way around it."

The pumps throbbed like giant hearts all through the stillness in the council chambers. The faces along the line of desks were smoothing out; the terror in them was fading away.

"And yet the Earth is almost dead," said Michael quietly, "and you can't bring it back to life."

"The sins of our past, Mr. Nelson," said the President. "The Atomic wars five thousand years ago. And the greed. It was too late a long time ago. That, of course, is why the expedition was sent out. And now you've come back to us with this terrible news." He looked around, slowly, then back to Michael. "Can you give us any hope at all?"

"None."

"Another expedition? To Andromeda perhaps? With you the leader?"

Michael shook his head. "We're finished with expeditions, Mr. President."

There were mutterings in the council, and hastily whispered consultations. Now they were watching the man and woman again.

"We feel," said the President, "it would be dangerous to allow you to go out among the people. They've been informed that your statement wasn't entirely true. This was necessary, to avoid a panic. The people simply must not know the whole truth." He paused. "Now we ask you to keep in mind that whatever we decide about the two of you will be for the good of the people."

Michael and Mary were silent.

"You'll wait outside the council chambers," the President went on, "until we have reached our decision."

As the man and woman were led away, the pumps beat in the stillness, and at the edge of the shrinking seas the salt thick waters were being pulled into the distilleries, and from them into the tier upon tier of artificial gardens that sat like giant bee hives all around the shoreline; and the mounds of salt glistening in the sunlight behind the gardens were growing into mountains.

---

In their rooms, Michael and Mary were talking through the hours, and waiting. All around them were fragile, form-fitting chairs and translucent walls and a ceiling that, holding the light of the sun when they had first seen it, was now filled with moonlight.

Standing at a circular window, ten feet in diameter, Michael saw, far below, the lights of the city extending into the darkness along the shoreline of the sea.

"We should have delivered our message by radio," he said, "and gone back into space."

"You could probably still go," she said quietly.

He came and stood beside her. "I couldn't stand being out in space, or anywhere, without you."

She looked up at him. "We could go out into the wilderness, Michael, outside the force walls. We could go far away."

He turned from her. "It's all dead. What would be the use?"

"I came from the Earth," she said quietly. "And I've got to go back to it. Space is so cold and frightening. Steel walls and blackness and the rockets and the little pinpoints of light. It's a prison."

"But to die out there in the desert, in that dust." Then he paused and looked away from her. "We're crazy—talking as though we had a choice."

"Maybe they'll have to *give* us a choice."

"What're you talking about?"

"They went into hysterics at the sight of those bodies in the picture. Those young bodies that didn't die of old age."

He waited.

"They can't stand the sight of people dying violently."

Her hand went to her throat and touched the tiny locket.

"These lockets were given to us so we'd have a choice between suffering or quick painless death.... We still have a choice."

He touched the locket at his own throat and was very still for a long moment. "So we threaten to kill ourselves, before their eyes. What would it do to them?"

He was still for a long time. "Sometimes, Mary, I think I don't know you at all." A pause. "And so now you and I are back where we started. Which'll it be, space or Earth?"

"Michael." Her voice trembled. "I—I don't know how to say this."

He waited, frowning, watching her intently.

"I'm—going to have a child."

His face went blank.

Then he stepped forward and took her by the shoulders. He saw the softness there in her face; saw her eyes bright as though the sun were shining in them; saw a flush in her cheeks, as though she had been running. And suddenly his throat was full.

"No," he said thickly. "I can't believe it."

"It's true."

He held her for a long time, then he turned his eyes aside.

"Yes, I can see it is."

"I—I can't put into words why I let it happen, Michael."

He shook his head. "I don't know—what to—to say. It's so incredible."

"Maybe—I got so—tired—just seeing the two of us over and over again and the culturing of the scar tissue, for twenty centuries. Maybe that was it. It was just—something I felt I *had* to do. Some—*real* life again. Something new. I felt a need to produce something out of myself. It all started way out in space, while we were getting close to the solar system. I began to wonder if we'd ever get out of the ship alive or if we'd ever see a sunset again or a dawn or the night or morning like we'd seen on Earth—so—so long ago. And then I *had* to let it happen. It was a vague and strange thing. There was something forcing me. But at the same time I wanted it, too. I seemed to be willing it, seemed to be feeling it was a necessary thing." She paused, frowning. "I didn't stop to think—it would be like this."

"Such a thing," he said, smiling grimly, "hasn't happened on Earth for three thousand years. I can remember in school, reading in the history books, how the whole Earth was overcrowded and how the food and water had to be rationed and then how the laws were passed forbidding birth and after that how the people died and there weren't any more babies born, until at last there was plenty of what the Earth had to give, for everyone. And then the news was broken to everyone about the culturing of the scar tissue, and there were a few dissenters but they were soon conditioned out of their dissension and the population was stabilized." He paused. "After all this past history, I don't think the council could endure what you've done."

"No," she said quietly. "I don't think they could."

"And so this will be just for *us*." He took her in his arms. "If I remember rightly, this is a traditional action." A pause. "Now I'll go with you out onto the Earth—if we can swing it. When we get outside the city, or if we do—Well, we'll see."

They were very still together and then he turned and stood by the window and looked down upon the city and she came and stood beside him.

---

They both saw it at the same time. And they watched, without speaking, both knowing what was in the other's mind and heart. They watched the giant four dimensional screens all through the city. A green, lush planet showed bright and clear on them and there were ships standing among the trees and men walking through the grass, that moved gently like the swells on a calm ocean, while into their minds came the thoughts projected from the screen:

"This will be your new home. It was found and then lost. But another expedition will be sent out to find it again. Be of good hope. Everything will be all right."

Michael turned from the window. "So there's our evidence. Two thousand years. All the others killed getting it. And with a simple twist, it becomes a lie."

Mary sat down and buried her face in her hands.

"What a terrible failure there's been here," said Michael. "The neglect and destruction of a whole planet. It's like a family letting their home decay all around them, and living in smaller and smaller rooms of it, until at last the rooms are all gone, and since they can't find another home, they all die in the ruins of the last room."

"I can't face dying," Mary said quietly, "squeezed in with all these people, in this tomb they've made around the seas. I want to have the open sky and the quiet away from those awful pounding pumps when I die. I want the spread of the Earth all around and the clean air. I want to be a real part of the Earth again."

Michael barely nodded in agreement. He was standing very still now.

And then there was the sound of the door opening.

They both rose, like mourners at a funeral, and went into the council chambers.

---

Again they sat in the thick chairs before the wall of desks with the faces of the council looking across it like defenders.

The pumps were beating, beating all through the room and the quiet.

The President was standing. He faced Michael and Mary, and seemed to set himself as though to deliver a blow, or to receive one.

"Michael and Mary," he said, his voice struggling against a tightness, "we've considered a long time concerning what is to be done with you and the report you brought back to us from the galaxy." He took another swallow of water. "To protect the sanity of the people, we've changed your report. We've also decided that the people must be protected from the possibility of your spreading the truth, as you did at the landing field. So, for the good of the people, you'll be isolated. All comforts will be given you. After all, in a sense, you *are* heroes and martyrs. Your scar tissue will be cultured as it has been in the past, and you will stay in solitary confinement until the time when, perhaps, we can migrate to another planet. We feel that hope must not be destroyed. And so another expedition is being sent out. It may be that, in time, on another planet, you'll be able to take your place in our society."

He paused. "Is there anything you wish to say?"

"Yes, there is."

"Proceed."

Michael stared straight at the President. After a long moment, he raised his hand to the tiny locket at his throat.

"Perhaps you remember," he said, "the lockets given to every member of the expedition the night before we left. I still have mine." He raised it. "So does my wife. They were designed to kill the wearer instantly and painlessly if he were ever faced with pain or a terror he couldn't endure."

The President was standing again. A stir ran along the barricade of desks.

"We can't endure the city," went on Michael, "or its life and the ways of the people." He glanced along the line of staring faces.

"If what I think you're about to say is true," said the President in a shaking voice, "it would have been better if you'd never been born."

"Let's face facts, Mr. President. We were *born* and haven't died—yet." A pause. "And we can kill ourselves right here before your eyes. It'd be painless to us. We'd be unconscious. But there would be horrible convulsions and grimaces. Our bodies would be twisted and torn. They'd thresh about. The deaths you saw in the picture happened a long time ago, in outer space. You all went into hysterics at the sight of them. Our deaths now would be close and terrible to see."

The President staggered as though about to faint. There was a stirring and muttering and a jumping up along the desks. Voices cried out, in anger and fear. Arms waved and fists pounded. Hands clasped and unclasped and clawed at collars, and there was a pell mell rushing around the President. They yelled at each other and clasped each other by the shoulders, turned away and back again, and then suddenly became very still.

Now they began to step down from the raised line of desks, the President leading them, and came close to the man and woman, gathering around them in a wide half circle.

Michael and Mary were holding the lockets close to their throats. The half circle of people, with the President at its center was moving closer and closer. They were sweaty faces and red ones and dry white ones and hands were raised to seize them.

Michael put his arm around Mary's waist. He felt the trembling in her body and the waiting for death.

"Stop!" he said quietly.

They halted, in slight confusion, barely drawing back.

"If you want to see us die—just come a step closer.... And remember what'll happen to you."

The faces began turning to each other and there was an undertone of muttering and whispering. "A ghastly thing.... Instant.... Nothing to do.... Space's broken their minds.... They'll do it.... Eyes're mad.... What can we do?... What?..." The sweaty faces, the cold white ones, the flushed hot ones: all began to turn to the President, who was staring at the two before him like a man watching himself die in a mirror.

"I command you," he suddenly said, in a choked voice, "to—to give me those—lockets! It's your—duty!"

"We've only one duty, Mr. President," said Michael sharply. "To ourselves."

"You're sick. Give yourselves over to us. We'll help you."

"We've made our choice. We want an answer. Quickly! Now!"

The President's body sagged. "What—what is it you want?"

Michael threw the words. "To go beyond the force fields of the city. To go far out onto the Earth and live as long as we can, and then to die a natural death."

The half circle of faces turned to each other and muttered and whispered again. "In the name of God.... Let them go.... Contaminate us.... Like animals.... Get them out of here.... *Let* them be finished.... Best for us all.... And them...."

There was a turning to the President again and hands thrusting him forward to within one step of Michael and Mary, who were standing there close together, as though attached.

Haltingly he said, "Go. Please go. Out onto the Earth—to die. You *will* die. The Earth is dead out there. You'll never see the city or your people again."

"We want a ground car," said Michael. "And supplies."

"A ground car," repeated the President. "And—supplies.... Yes."

"You can give us an escort, if you want to, out beyond the first range of mountains."

"There will be no escort," said the President firmly. "No one has been allowed to go out upon the Earth or to fly above it for many hundreds of years. We know it's there. That's enough. We couldn't bear the sight of it." He took a step back. "And we can't bear the sight of you any longer. Go now. Quickly!"

Michael and Mary did not let go of the lockets as they watched the half circle of faces move backward, staring, as though at corpses that should sink to the floor.

---

It was night. The city had been lost beyond the dead mounds of Earth that rolled away behind them, like a thousand ancient tombs. The ground car sat still on a crumbling road.

Looking up through the car's driving blister, they saw the stars sunk into the blue black ocean of space; saw the path of the Milky Way along which they had rushed, while they had been searching frantically for the place of salvation.

"If any one of the other couples had made it back," said Mary, "do you think they'd be with us?"

"I think they'd either be with us," he said, "or out in space again—or in prison."

She stared ahead along the beam of headlight that stabbed out into the night over the decaying road.

"How sorry are you," she said quietly, "coming with me?"

"All I know is, if I were out in space for long without you, I'd kill myself."

"Are we going to die out here, Michael?" she said, gesturing toward the wall of night that stood at the end of the headlight, "with the land?"

He turned from her, frowning, and drove the ground car forward, watching the headlights push back the darkness.

They followed the crumbling highway all night until light crept across the bald and cracked hills. The morning sun looked down upon the desolation ten feet above the horizon when the car stopped. They sat for a long time then, looking out upon the Earth's parched and inflamed skin. In the distance a wall of mountains rose like a great pile of bleached bones. Close ahead the rolling plains were motionless waves of dead Earth with a slight breeze stirring up little swirls of dust.

"I'm getting out," she said.

"I haven't the slightest idea how much farther to go, or why," said Michael shrugging. "It's all the same. Dirt and hills and mountains and sun and dust. It's really not much different from being out in space. We live in the car just like in a space ship. We've enough concentrated supplies to last for a year. How far do we go? Why? When?"

They stepped upon the Earth and felt the warmth of the sun and strolled toward the top of the hill.

"The air smells clean," he said.

"The ground feels good. I think I'll take off my shoes." She did. "Take off your boots, Michael. Try it."

Wearily he pulled off his boots, stood in his bare feet. "It takes me back."

"Yes," she said and began walking toward the hilltop.

He followed, his boots slung around his neck. "There was a road somewhere, with the dust between my toes. Or was it a dream?"

"I guess when the past is old enough," she said, "it becomes a dream."

He watched her footprints in the dust. "God, listen to the quiet."

"I can't seem to remember so much quiet around me. There's always been the sound of a space ship, or the pumps back in the cities."

He did not answer but continued to watch her footsteps and to feel the dust squishing up between his toes. Then suddenly:

"Mary!"

She stopped, whirling around.

He was staring down at her feet.

She followed his gaze.

"It's grass!" He bent down. "Three blades."

She knelt beside him. They touched the green blades.

"They're new," he said.

They stared, like religious devotees concentrating upon some sacred object.

He rose, pulling her up with him. They hurried to the top of the hill and stood very still, looking down into a valley. There were tiny patches of green and little trees sprouting, and here and there, a pale flower. The green was in a cluster, in the center of the valley and there was a tiny glint of sunlight in its center.

"Oh!"

Her hand found his.

They ran down the gentle slope, feeling the patches of green touch their feet, smelling a new freshness in the air. And coming to the little spring, they stood beside it and watched the crystal water that trickled along the valley floor and lost itself around a bend. They saw a furry, little animal scurry away and heard the twitter of a bird and saw it resting on a slim, bending branch. They heard the buzz of a bee, saw it light on a pale flower at their feet and work at the sweetness inside.

Mary knelt down and drank from the spring.

"It's so cool. It must come from deep down."

"It does," he said. There were tears in his eyes and a tightness in his throat. "From deep down."

"We can *live* here, Michael!"

Slowly he looked all around until his sight stopped at the bottom of a hill. "We'll build our house just beyond those rocks. We'll dig and plant and you'll have the child."

"Yes!" she said. "Oh yes!"

"And the ones back in the city will know the Earth again. Sometime we'll lead them back here and show them the Earth is coming alive." He paused. "By following what we had to do for ourselves, we've found a way to save them."

They remained kneeling in the silence beside the pool for a long time. They felt the sun on their backs and looked into the clean depth of the water deeply aware of the new life breathing all around them and of themselves absorbing it, and at the same time giving back to it the life that was their own.

There was only this quiet and breathing and warmth until Michael stood and picked up a rock and walked toward the base of the hill where he had decided to build the house.

Milton Keynes UK
Ingram Content Group UK Ltd.
UKHW030744071024
449371UK00006B/555